*Do Not Go Naked
into Your Next Presentation*

D0110734

DO NOT GO

NAKED

INTO YOUR NEXT

PRESENTATION

*Nifty Little Nuggets to Quiet the Nerves
and Please the Crowd*

RON HOFF

ANDREWS AND McMEEL
A UNIVERSAL PRESS SYNDICATE COMPANY
KANSAS CITY

Library of Congress Cataloging-in-Publication Data
Hoff, Ron.
Do not go naked into your next presentation: nifty little nuggets to quiet the nerves and please the crowd / by Ron Hoff.
    p. cm.
  ISBN 0-8362-2713-1 (pbk.)
  1. Public speaking. I. Title.
PN4121.H454 1997
808.5′ 1—dc20   96-46193
                                    CIP

◄ Contents ►

◄ Prologue ►

"Alas . . . The Speaker Has No Clothes"

The speaker has just been introduced, but is nowhere to be seen. (Oh, here he comes now . . . bustling down the aisle, looking at his watch.)

As he hustles up the wooden stairs to the platform, a page of manuscript flutters to the floor. The speaker doesn't see it. A Good Samaritan in the first row comes foward, picks up the wayward page, and hands it to the speaker. Not understanding exactly where the page belongs in his loosely assembled manuscript, the speaker places it on the rostrum, apart from the rest of his script. The audience gets its first small hint that all is not well.

Meanwhile, the speaker is getting oriented to his surroundings. Papers crackle in the public address system. The speaker looks up and says to no one in particular, "Does anyone know how to turn on the slide projector?" No answer. More crackling noises.

The audience does what audiences always do when something isn't quite right. They twist around and stare at the back of the room, as if expecting an army of technicians to come marching to the rescue. No. Not this time. The speaker seems to be on his own.

Suddenly the screen behind the speaker explodes into a blinding flash of whiteness. The projector is working, but there's nothing in it. "Does anybody know where my slides are?" There is a slight tremble in the speaker's voice this time. The screen clicks to black for a split second and explodes to whiteness again. Another blank. The slides are *definitely* missing.

As the speaker cups his hand to shield his eyes from the searing white light, the truth dawns upon the audience. *The speaker has no clothes.* The realization spreads like a small electric shock. The speaker hasn't even started his presentation and he has been clearly revealed for what he is. Unprepared, unrehearsed, unaware of what to do next, and getting *very* nervous.

*

The purpose of *Do Not Go Naked into Your Next Presentation* is to give you everything you need in order for you to feel confident and fearless the next time you get up to speak. That means every little thing—from when is the best time of day for you to speak, to when is the *worst* (near the cocktail hour). Other nuggets that can be invaluable to you: How an audience will size you up *in a minute*. Should you give a softball or a hardball speech? (There's a big difference.) Ten tips to follow in picking a subject. The secret of coming up with a great title. And many, many more. Quick bursts of energy. Insights and information. Little things mostly, but terribly important to the overall impression you'll make.

This book is your new suit of clothes for your next presentation. Try on the first few pages and see how they fit.

RON HOFF

I

"Up-front"
Discoveries

Twelve years of professional speaking, from Calgary to Key West to Sardinia, have enabled me to discover a treasure of "nuggets" that would dress up any speaker's kitbag. Here are thirty-three for your next presentation.

◂ 1 ▸
Be First!

If you can be first, be first.

Next best is last. (More about that shortly.)

When you're first, you can be fairly sure that you'll start on time. (At least, you'll eliminate the possibility of coming on after the presenters before you have all run overtime and completely screwed up the schedule.)

When you're first, the audience is fresh. But, more important, *you're* fresh. The first speaker always has the edge. And the audience is listening because nobody has numbed its brain.

If you start somewhere in the middle of the program, you'll be at the mercy of *everything*—the clock, the quality of air in the room, the inertia level that has been created by preceding speakers. Don't let somebody else lull your audience into a state of semiconsciousness if you can possibly avoid it.

Being *last* is second best to being *first* because you can sum up what everybody else has said and maybe draw some insights that will bring your audience to life. Also most audiences will give the last speaker a little extra attention because they're so grateful there are no more speeches.

◀ 2 ▶

After Five

Never, ever allow yourself to be scheduled to speak after 5:00 P.M. That's too close to the cocktail hour.

After-dinner speakers are a special breed, used to dealing with clattering dishes and chattering guests. They have ad libs for *any* accident. They enjoy squashing hecklers. They are impervious to noise.

Unless *nothing* bothers you—or you have aspirations to be a stand-up comic—don't speak after sunset.

◀ 3 ▶

All Communication Is Local

When you get right down to it, right down to the bedrock basis of any piece of communication, the audience is sitting there thinking, "Now where does this subject fit into my life?"

Most audiences will conclude—after a *very* few minutes—that the speaker doesn't know beans about the audience's life.

Result: There's no possibility of a connection.

Here's an idea: Check into town twenty-four hours early. Spend as many hours as possible walking around, talking to people, asking questions about the organization you'll be addressing the next day. Listen to the local radio station. Read the local newspaper and tuck it under your arm when you get up to speak. Then, pepper that speech of yours with local references. Let your audience know that you took the trouble to find out about their town and their lives. You'll be amazed at the interest they'll suddenly take in you.

◄ 4 ►
The Unshakable Truth

Presentation starts with content. The cool, clear substance of what you want to communicate.

When content disintegrates or fails to make sense, delivery suffers.

Delivery alone, no matter how dramatic, cannot carry a presentation.

If you want to improve your delivery, crank up your content.

Monologues in the Lobby

FIRST LADY: Did you see my son's picture in the Sunday *Tribune*? He was just made an associate professor of . . .

SECOND LADY: You know, I started to read the *Trib*, but I suddenly remembered the recipe I promised the kids I would make—rhubarb pie.

FIRST LADY: I was so proud of him. He's worked so hard for that position—and, frankly, so have we.

SECOND LADY: You know, when I got into it, it turned out to be more like a cake than a pie—but it was pink and it tasted like rhubarb.

FIRST LADY: Well, I'll save a copy of the *Tribune* for you. We bought quite a few extra copies.

*

Many presentations are like the conversation I overheard in the lobby of my condominium. The presenter talks about his or her interest—and is consumed by it.

The audience is thinking about something else and can't let go of it.

At the end, the conversation has really been two monologues.

As a speaker, you have to put yourself in the shoes of your audience—or make your subject so fascinating that the audience will want to get into your shoes. It's much easier to do the former than the latter.

◄ 6 ►
Their Problems Can Cure Yours

Take my word for this—
You're never going to know too much about your audience or what they're concerned about. The more you know about their problems, the less you'll worry about your own.

◄ 7 ►
The Designated Expert

When you're a speaker, you are a designated expert. People who aren't experts don't get asked to make speeches.

So, you can tell yourself—and mean it—that you know more about your subject than anybody else in the room.

That shouldn't make you arrogant.

But it does entitle you to a strong point of view.

This point of view will steer almost everything you say. It should be stated early, and often. There must be nothing ambivalent about it. You have chipped it out of stone. It is emblematic of your expertness.

A presenter who waltzes around a subject without a point of view isn't an expert. A fancy dancer, maybe, but not an expert.

◄ 8 ►
Something to Think About

Before you can define your point of view on the subject to be addressed, you'll have to define yourself.

Most people never do that in a lifetime.

◄ 9 ►
Win / Win

Keep this little nugget in mind all the way through the speech-making process:

BEFORE your presentation, you are taking care of yourself. You are getting your brain ready, doing your research. You are getting your body ready, working with the props you will use. You are getting your nerves ready, anticipating the questions that may come up.

DURING your presentation, you are taking care of your audience. You are applying everything you have learned to their needs, their problems, their questions. You are there for them, for whatever help you can provide.

Before you speak, take care of yourself.

When you speak, take care of your audience.

It's a win/win proposition.

◄ 10 ►
"Wish I May, Wish I Might Have the Wish I Wish Tonight."

Remember that?

People come to conferences hoping that they will get *one* idea from each speech—one idea they can put to work in their own lives.

Research shows that they are severely disappointed. In fact, 49 percent of all speeches are regarded as failures—empty of *any* ideas.

So, if you can impart one usable idea to every member of your audience, you will be hailed as *more* than a great speaker. You will be acclaimed as somebody who actually took the pains to understand the needs of the audience.

◄ 11 ►

The Audience Looks at You and Says, "I Know Who You Are."

M ost audiences have open minds. But they also have quick minds. Here's what I mean:

When you start your speech, the audience is inclined to give you every benefit of the doubt. Every audience has a "wish" (note preceding page), and it's hoping that you are the embodiment of that wish. If you are, the audience will say, "I know who you are. You are the speaker who has an idea I can really use."

That realization comes quickly. But other realizations can also come quickly.

- ◄ "I know who you are. You're a hopeless bore."
- ◄ "I know who you are. You're just trying to stir up a little business for yourself."
- ◄ "I know who you are. You're a wannabe comic."

Every audience has a *sixth sense* that detects the conclusion to "I know who you are . . ." and it is unfailingly accurate. Before you get up to make your speech, write exactly how you want to be perceived by that particular audience. There's no trick to this. Just one requirement: *What you write . . . better be true.*

◄ 12 ►
Selecting a Subject

1. Pick a subject that absolutely fascinates you. You'd be reading about it on a beach somewhere if you weren't scheduled to be giving a speech.
2. Pick a subject that you have spoken about before. You've got a good file on it.
3. Pick a subject that prompts recollections from the past. Good, meaty memories. A cardboard box of old photographs is usually a good place to start.
4. Pick a subject that will touch everybody in your audience.
5. Pick a subject that you have experienced *firsthand*. It's not enough to go to the library. Pick something that happened *to you* and had a lasting impact.
6. Pick a subject that is essentially *simple*. It shouldn't have a lot of plots and subplots.
7. Pick a subject that has a little controversy in it, but don't pick one that will start a fistfight. (That is, unless you run a daytime "talk show.")
8. Pick a subject from *your journal*, if you keep one. If you don't, start keeping one. It will reward you with a treasure trove of speaking subjects.

9. Pick a subject that has "picture postcards" in it. That is, it prompts instant visuals.

10. Pick a subject that has been suggested by your host or hostess, but make it *yours*. Put some pictures of your kids in it. It *never* fails.

◂ 13 ▸
The Secret of Titles

Here's the secret of titles: Whatever kind of speech you're making, pretend that you are making it in competition with four other speeches that will be held at exactly the same time as yours. Actually, this arrangement is quite popular; the simultaneous speeches are called "break-out" sessions.

The attendees at the conference or convention pick *one* "break-out" speech to visit. It's a kind of popularity contest—only everything depends on the title.

Here's how to get *everybody* into your speech.

Give your title some teeth, and a bit of greed. Front load it with a benefit, and add a specific figure (preferably with a dollar sign in front of it). Let me show you how this works:

HOW TO OPEN YOUR OWN BUSINESS
AND MAKE $75,000 YOUR FIRST YEAR.

Don't let anybody tell you it's too long. Don't let anybody tell you it should be "cuter." The title above comes with a guarantee: You'll outdraw every speaker in the place or I'll send you back whatever you paid for this book.

◄ 14 ►
The Defining Difference

Critics have a line they just love to use. "Interesting . . . but it doesn't bring anything new to the subject."

It's a painful criticism, but it suggests a question that you'll have to face, sooner or later: "What's the defining difference in my speech?"

Think about it. See if you can write it down in a bare minimum of words. Is it really a discrete concept? Have you really brought something fresh and provocative to the party?

Don't give yourself that tired, old dodge, "Well, it may not be revolutionary—but it's certainly something they need to be reminded of."

That may be, but your audience is not going to remember you as having given them a great *reminder* speech.

There *aren't* any great reminder speeches.

◄ 15 ►

Listen! The Room
Is Talking to You.

Take the time to get acquainted with the room that will play host to your presentation. Stand in the middle of it by yourself, and see if you can make contact with it.

Understand that a room absorbs all of the meetings that have ever taken place in it. As a result, it exudes an atmosphere that can be warm or chilly, friendly or distant.

Not long ago, I spoke in an old church in Portland, Oregon. It hadn't been used for a long time. It had heavy, oaken beams and windows with milky glass that diffused the light into a kind of haze. But the thing that I remember most was the *dust*. The dust was overwhelming.

There were about 300 people sitting there. As I looked out into the room, they reminded me of ghosts—with the filtered light from the windows backlighting the figures in the pews.

When my presentation began, I could barely see the people sitting in the back rows. I walked down the aisle toward them, wondering if I could find my way back. I looped around behind my audience, talking all the while, thinking I should be dropping tiny pebbles or something. It was eerie. My easels and electronic paraphernalia seemed strangely out of place. I felt like a pied piper trying to attract followers in a mausoleum.

At the end of my presentation, the people got up and filed past me. I nodded at them, they nodded at me, as if the funeral were over.

Finally, when the church was absolutely empty, I could feel its dignity. I looked around and thought, "You win." It was really no contest.

When you speak out of town, be sure to ask for a full description of the room. Find out if it's cheery or dark, open or cavernous. See if you can determine its personality, sight unseen, then check it out carefully when you arrive.

If you're going to speak in a dinner theater, you can expect great audiovisual support, but it's going to be crowded with tables and chairs. And the technicians will be inclined to spotlight you like a lounge act.

If you're going to speak in a school, you can expect your room to be rectangular and bright—probably with rickety equipment. The chairs will be uncomfortable for adults and you will inevitably become "the teacher." Don't resist. Pick up some chalk and move among "your students."

If you're going to speak in a room designed for business presentations in a conference center—with amphitheater seating arrangements, lights that have been installed by an expert in theater lighting, and a technician operating the multimedia stuff—you can expect as good a response as your material warrants.

The conditions of your speaking environment make a tremendous difference. Don't let anyone downplay their importance when you are setting up.

Insist upon controlling the arrangements in the room so that you and your environment can be as compatible as possible. The room will give you its signals. You will do well to listen carefully.

◄ 16 ►
Whatever It Is,
It's Your Responsibility

So the door is open at the back of the hall and makes a loud, moaning noise every time somebody goes in or out. Get the maintenance man to give it a shot of oil.

So the phone rings. Appoint somebody to answer it—or remove the phone before the meeting begins.

So you have a heckler. Usher him or her out the door. Be firm. Don't hesitate to ask someone who knows the heckler to give you a hand.

If you are conducting a seminar or holding a major meeting, everything that happens inside that room is your responsibility. When something goes wrong, don't wait for somebody else to know what to do. Take charge. Get the damn thing fixed.

When you present, you lead.

◄ 17 ►
You'll Never Miss with "You"

If you're reading this in an airplane on your way to make a speech somewhere, and you've come to the conclusion that your talk just doesn't connect—pick a number.

How about eighteen?

Tell yourself you are going to inject the word "you" into your script eighteen times.

Then, get your pencil working, adding little "hooks" like these:

◄ "Now what does that mean to *you*?"
◄ "Have *you* ever asked yourself that question?"
◄ "Does that sound interesting to *you*?"
◄ "Let's bring *you* into this equation . . ."
◄ "*You* may be saying this doesn't mean a damn thing to me."
◄ "Do *you* ever feel that way?"

◄ "It's time for *you* to vote *yes* or *no*—"

◄ "What do *you* say?"

◄ "Can *you* help me on this?"

Already, we've got nine "you's" working to increase the connective impact of your speech. In the process of putting in the "you's," we have obligated *you* to explain your subject in terms that your audience is going to find *much* more involving.

"You" is the most personal word in the English language. Only one word comes closer: the name of the person you're talking to.

◄ 18 ►
David Belasco Test

The simpler the idea for your speech, the better your speech will be. David Belasco said that the idea for every play he ever produced could be written as one simple sentence on the back of his business card. Could your speech pass David Belasco's test? Try it on the next page.

◄ 19 ►
All Presentations
Are Competitive

There is no such thing as a routine presentation. Every time you step up, you are presenting *the sum total of what you are*. You are always being compared with somebody—often the speakers who preceded you.

That is why it's always a good idea to be in the audience when the speakers before you are presenting themselves. Rate them. Be tough. Then, get up and raise the standard.

◄ 20 ►

"Facts Never Speak for Themselves"

—Alfred Marshall, nineteenth-century economist

Is Mr. Marshall hopelessly wrong?

Think about it for a minute . . .

Consider the last court trial you saw. Or the last debate on TV. Or the last argument in the halls of Congress. Often the same, identical set of facts can add up to *two* uniquely different stories when presented by two people.

The facts, laid bare—as they say—probably aren't worth much until somebody verifies them, clarifies them, certifies them, interprets them, *presents* them.

When you have collected the facts, your task of presentation has really just begun. The audience will vote on how you *see* the facts.

◄ 21 ►
The Killer Question

Most of us are called upon to make a sales presentation at some time in our lives. Some of us spend our whole lives making sales presentations—linking the client's unique need to our unique product. Or trying to.

Good salespeople make the linkage. *But what happens when you don't have a unique product to meet the prospect's unique need?* That's the killer question. You have a *commodity* product—just like everybody else's product.

Here's the answer: *You* become the uniqueness in the product. The service that *only you can provide* becomes the point of difference in the product. One word of caution: The prospect better recognize that difference quickly or your entire presentation, product, *and* presenter, becomes generic.

That's when the fat lady sings.

◄ 22 ►
The Easiest Sale

So many speakers see themselves as enlightened evangelists, messengers with magical answers.

Most audiences aren't looking for far-out solutions.

They'd much rather hear about something they have long suspected to be true. The easiest sale is going to be made to the CEO who says, "You know, that's what I've been thinking all along."

◄ 23 ►
Let the Speech Fit the Site

If you're going to give an instructional talk on how to conduct a safety seminar, you should be in a smallish room.

After all, you've got a smallish subject. You'll look like an idiot talking about safety seminars in a chandeliered ballroom just before a six-course dinner.

By the same token, you don't want to deliver a landmark speech on global warming in a committee room that holds twelve people.

I admit this sounds like pretty obvious stuff, but I do have an explanation: Guess who made the little safety speech in the chandeliered ballroom?

◂ 24 ▸
Joy

At some point in your presentation, your audience should see something in you that they haven't noticed before: A feeling of exhilaration.

You don't have to do anything theatrical to show your joy.

Maybe a member of your audience suddenly changes from a "lump" to an energetic participant. Maybe he suddenly *gets* what you've been struggling to show him. He comes to life, jubilant about his discovery. You can share that jubilation with him.

Maybe the whole room changes. It becomes attentive, even engrossed. You have ignited a spark that didn't exist before. The questions are no longer testing you. People are volunteering all over the place. It's a joyful, awakening time!

So why not celebrate? The act of bonding with people is one of the most joyful experiences in life. It doesn't happen all that often in a business meeting or seminar. So, when it does, whoop it up.

◄ 25 ►
Second Thoughts

When addressing any group, listen to your "second thoughts" before you say anything critical.

An old boss of mine used to say, "Never complain, never explain." It took me a while to fully understand that bit of wisdom . . . never find fault, never make excuses.

◄ 26 ►
Mr. Research

My grandson Sam.

If you've got a picture of a grandson—or a daughter, or a niece—make a slide of the kid and finesse it into your presentation.

> *"I tried the idea on my number-one
> research aide this morning. He was
> busy on another project, but he's always
> got something to say."*

Be prepared for people to come up afterward and say, "You know, I've got a kid just like yours at home."

◄ 27 ►

Package Your Talking Points

A youthful minister just north of Lake Geneva, Wisconsin, was preparing his sermon for the following Sunday.

He was seated in an office chair that could rotate a full 360 degrees.

The walls of his office were covered with scraps of paper. A handwritten line or two was Magic Markered on each scrap. His computer screen blinked in front of him. His printer was chunking out copies of hand-printed headlines on colored stock behind him. Now, he even had pieces of colored paper stuck to the computer screen.

"These are all my talking points," he said, clipping a picture from a recent magazine. He stuck it on one of the few empty spots on the wall in front of him.

"I'll use some of these ideas, hold others in the back of my mind. In a minute, I'll get them organized—but not *too* organized. I like things a little bit abstract."

There must have been seventy-five squares of colored paper on the four walls. It looked as if someone had shot off a cannon. He had his scissors going again, cutting up strips of paper, all of them yellow. He'd write a word or two in green on each strip.

"Each strip of paper makes an important point," he said, daubing the strips with rubber cement. He clustered the colored Post-its under the strips, stopping only occasionally to move a square or reposition a clipping.

"You see, the secret of my system is to make everything movable. Nothing's static anymore. You don't sit down and write a speech on a sheet of paper, page after page, with everything nicely numbered and totally boring.

"You put colored squares on the walls so that you become a part of the script, and the whole thing revolves around you. When I get up to make my sermon this Sunday, I'll see pretty much what you see here. Talking points that are alive, forming different patterns inside my head."

He whirled a full 360 degrees in his chair.

◄ 28 ►
Taking Notes

There's nothing wrong with telling your audience when and where to take notes as you proceed through your speech.

"You might want to make a note of this . . ."

Most people will do exactly what you suggest.

Just make sure that you slow the tempo a bit to give them enough time to write what you tell them to write.

More importantly, make sure that the notes they take are worth keeping.

◄ 29 ►
Ninety Seconds

People are going to reach their conclusions about you as a speaker with terrifying speed. Within the first ninety seconds. A keeper or a turkey.

◄ 30 ►
A Little Joke

Nothing ever happens between two people until some-body gets excited. If the two "people" we're talking about are *you* and *your audience*, you can be absolutely certain that your audience will not be excited first.

◄ 31 ►
Transference

He looked like a perfectly nice man—neatly trimmed mus-tache, fluffy hair.

He was the Secretary of the Navy during the Tailhook sexual misconduct scandal (1991). His name, for the record, was H. Lawrence Garrett III—and, after his resignation, one headline seemed to sum up all of his efforts to keep the navy under control:

"He led those who would not follow."

Apparently, Garrett never understood the difference between giving orders and a little-known technique of persuasion called *transference*.

◄ Orders are issued in a stern voice to people who are *sup-posed* to follow. There's no art to it. It's all very cut-and-dried. *"Don't* do this . . ." *"Do* this . . ." Orders are seldom, if ever, issued in terms to make them appear rational to the followers.

◄ Transference is transferring orders into a follower's self-interest. Transference is showing "those who would not follow" why it was in their best interest to follow. It never happened during Tailhook. The leaders didn't seem to believe their own orders about sexual rowdiness ("This *is* the Navy, after all.") and the followers weren't unlawful, they were simply unled.

Audiences seldom follow orders. And they don't sit still very long for cold facts (see nugget #20). Without transference, they just daydream and wait for the bar to open.

◄ 32 ►
Common Threads

Every audience wears its personal life pretty close to the surface. Make a connection with that personal life in a way that demonstrates you've lived through it, too—and you're home free.

My grandson's photograph on page 24 was always a big hit when I was talking to a group of young couples. Nothing tops having kids as a way of bonding with a bunch of parents.

If you've been asked to speak at your high school reunion, don't hesitate to lead the group in one great, resonating cheer that everybody remembers. It will be even more emotional if you were the head cheerleader and you throw a baton in the air. (You'll bring the house down if you catch it.)

If you're talking to a group of young business executives at a resort hotel, lead off with a Dilbert cartoon that reflects the humorous side of the situation you have been asked to discuss. If everybody laughs, you'll know you've hit a common thread.

Once you find that *emotional* button that everybody responds to, you're likely to be accepted on all other levels as well.

◄ 33 ►
March, Yes . . . To Where?

So often, it seems, audiences are *challenged*. They are given *big* missions. They are told to straighten their backbones and march to a different drummer.

And march they do.

Only they're not really sure of where they're going.

*

Recently, I had a similar sensation. I was attending a meeting sponsored by my insurance company. The speaker told me to get up off my butt and learn about hypertension—the silent killer. I was handed a little folder that directed me to my hospital, conveniently located on the other side of the town. I marched out, congratulating myself on attending the meeting, and dropped the folder in the trash. Later, I tried to think how the speaker might have handled his "bid for action."

*

"I have a registered nurse standing by in the back of the room to check your blood pressure and give you a detailed printout within three minutes. It's absolutely painless, and it won't cost you a cent."

If the audience didn't move fast enough, I'd say, "And for once in your life you'll do something your doctor would approve of. In fact, you may just cheat him out of an office call."

*

Here's how to get an audience to do what you want:

- ◄ Give them something specific *to do*, not something to think about.
- ◄ Furnish whatever equipment or supplies they'll need.
- ◄ Make the date as immediate as possible, not some time in the future.
- ◄ Give them a mission that offers a strong incentive, such as saving money.

Most speeches don't have a prayer of getting anybody to do anything. The messages run through the mind like rainwater down a gutter. The more *unavoidable* you can tailor the mission for your audience, the more likely the mission will be accomplished.

II

"Rehearse, Rehearse . . . but remember this: You're always a little bit dangerous."

You never want to rehearse the excitement out of your rehearsal. But, even when you're speaking on the edge, you've got to know what you're doing and where you're going.

◄ 34 ►
A Little Bit Dangerous

The best presenters I have ever seen all seemed just a little bit *dangerous* to me—even in rehearsals. You sensed that they might do something shocking or off-the-wall at any time. Like Jack Palance diving to the floor and doing one-arm push-ups at the Academy Awards.

◄ 35 ►
Settle on a Start

Settle on a terrific start and stick with it. If you fuss with your opening—even change it as you approach the speaking platform—your brain will be like a train careening down two sets of tracks. Give your mind one set of tracks and stay on it until your speech is safely "in the barn."

◄ 36 ►
Intensity

Intensity is like electric current, feeding from the speaker into the nervous system of the audience. With some particularly dynamic speakers, this can cause *discomfort* in the audience. But it is far better to have intensity and risk audience discomfort than *not* to have it and never make a connection.

◄ 37 ►
Mirrors

Give your presentation to a full-length mirror. Mirrors are wonderful critics. They don't exaggerate. They're discreet. And you can try anything in front of them and they never giggle.

◄ 38 ►
Rehearsing the Team

When a team is rehearsing for a major presentation to a group, be ready for some rather off-putting requests like these:

"I'll just sort of walk through my part. I'm still whipping it into shape."

Or—

"Let me just outline my part for you. It'll take less time than going through it word for word."

Or—

"When I do it *for real*, I'll give it everything I've got. But right now, I just don't feel up to it."

Here's the point to be made:

If a presenter doesn't want to rehearse with the rest of the team, maybe he or she shouldn't be on the team next time. That simple observation should produce a noticeable increase in energy level of the entire squad from that moment on.

◄ 39 ►
The Voice

The voice is a nonverbal form of communication. We think of it in association with words, but it is the sound and tone of the voice that people recognize and remember.

Consider the voices of:

Sean Connery	Peter Jennings
Oprah Winfrey	Barbara Walters
Orson Welles	Arnold Schwarzenegger
Michael Jordan	Diane Sawyer

What do you hear? Do you hear specific words being said by those voices—or do you simply hear the *sound* and *tone* of those voices?

Put your voice on an audiotape with any of the voices above—and make comparisons for sound and tone.

Most highly memorable voices have a humming sound that runs behind the words, imparting resonance.

Start humming and let words form as you continue to hum. Do it until you run out of breath, then try it again using different words. Vocal scales are practiced in much the same way—only the voice moves up and down the scale.

If this sounds too complicated for you, just concentrate on listening to the sound and tone of voices for a while. You'll hear that undertone (or hum) in the most interesting voices—and one of these days you may detect it in your own.

◄ 40 ►
Numbers

So many presentations are loaded with numbers. We see slide after slide of numbers. The speaker tries to explain all of them. The audience tries to keep up. It's exhausting.

Your job, as the presenter, is to *take us behind* the numbers. Tell us what they mean to us. Which ones point to a trend and which ones point to nowhere.

If the numbers keep showing up on markable surfaces, circle the numbers in vibrant colors that imply a crucial relationship—such as a green, red, or yellow.

When you say, "You can forget the numbers on this page, they're just for accountants," you are demonstrating your expertness—and providing a welcome service for your audience.

The secret of presenting numbers is simple: Identify the dead ones, bring the others to life, and keep summarizing.

At the end, write two or three crisp lines that crystallize everything. Your audience will breathe a sigh of relief. And you will be hailed as a brilliant analyst instead of a tiresome numbers cruncher.

The Little Things

It's Sunday morning. A dignified member of the congregation gets up to read the Scripture. The Bible is carefully tucked under his arm. The expression on the face is somber. The spine is straight. The walk to the podium is purposeful.

The congregation waits in silent expectation.

The Scripture reader opens the Bible to the marked page. He looks down. Silence. Heavy silence.

The Scripture reader leans forward, trying to see the words. He jerks at the lamp cord on the podium, hoping for a higher level of illumination.

There is no higher level—only "on" and "off."

The speaker holds the Bible up close to the tiny little bulb and bends closer. He's in trouble. He simply cannot see the words. His glasses reflect the glare of the tiny light.

He begins to read—hesitantly, haltingly. He can't read his text as he practiced. It's embarrassing. He stumbles through to the end.

As he leaves the platform, his head is down. His wife pats him on the back as he returns to the family pew.

One little rehearsal before church started and the whole sorry business could have been corrected. Even a penlight, tucked in the text, would have provided that little jolt of light that the Scripture needed.

Check "the little things." At the most awkward times, they can be *big* things.

◄ 42 ►

There's a Judge in the Hall

"Counsel, where are you going with this line of questioning?"

Ever wondered how often a business audience asks that question when listening to a speaker? How often have *you*, as a member of an audience, asked yourself, "Where on earth is this thing headed? I don't have the faintest notion."

There's danger lurking in those thoughts.

It isn't very far from, "I don't have the faintest notion," to, "I don't *care* where it's headed. I've *had it* with this speaker."

When you're rehearsing, pretend there's a tough-as-nails judge in your audience who *has to know* where you're going or you'll be hammered into your seat.

◄ 43 ►
A Good Story

It's hard to beat a good story, particularly one that relates to your audience:

> *This is a true story of*
> *an old sailing ship that*
> *was blown into the Bermuda*
> *Triangle one stormy night*
> *. . . the captain was a wily*
> *old sea dog who had three*
> *ways to handle terrible storms:*
> *It just so happens the one he chose*
> *that stormy night could*
> *also work miracles in your business.*

Now, who could resist that?

◄ 44 ►
Teachers

Teachers are such wonderful inspirations for speakers.

Recently, I asked a group of young people this question: "What one thing do you remember most vividly about your favorite teacher in high school?"

Faces lit up.

"I remember the voice of my civics teacher. It was so deep that everything he said sounded terribly important."

Then, a young woman spoke:

"I remember my world history teacher. She was eighty years old, white hair—and what I remember most vividly was the way she carried herself. When she moved around that classroom—so straight and tall—I could see her as the queen of England."

And then, from the rear of the room:

"I remember my math teacher—not for her voice or how she moved—but because she took more interest in me than anybody else I have ever known."

The room grew still. The third answer seemed to strike a chord in everybody. The *very* best teachers, everyone agreed, seem to be aware of everyone in the class as *individuals*—sensitive to their needs as individuals.

Great speakers have that same wonderful ability. They see an audience as *individuals*—each one worthy of special attention. When that happens—when each person feels that special interest has been shown—nobody in the room is going to forget the experience.

◄ 45 ►

People Lie:
Body Language, Never

Ever watch the "trash TV" shows in the afternoon? They are the best places in the world to learn *body language*.

See that outstretched leg with that waggling foot, constantly flipping back and forth? Something is being said that makes that person uncomfortable—yet there's an *arrogance* about that waggle. It's sending a signal: "Talk on. I'll do whatever I damn well please."

See that woman rub her hands across her eyes? She's trying to erase a "bad scene" that somebody else is trying to pin on her.

Who is that guy with his cap on backward and his arms folded high across his chest, and his legs splayed out in all directions. "Count me out of this," he's saying.

Make a videotape of yourself during rehearsal and read your own body language.

◄ 46 ►
Show Us

If there's a *noun* in your presentation, consider showing us what the noun represents. If you're talking about a book, *show us* the book. If you're talking about a typical consumer, *show us* a one-minute videotape of that consumer. If you're talking about a product, *show us* that product.

◄ 47 ►
The Only Audiovisual Cautions You Need to Know

1. Whatever audiovisual equipment you decide to take with you, just remember you'll have to carry it (unless you've hired help).

2. Don't use any audiovisual equipment that you don't know how to fix. If you're relying on the guy from the hotel where you're speaking, you're in trouble.

3. Don't use any audiovisual equipment unless you can use it with authority. If you seem uncertain about the equipment you're using, your audience will probably think you're shaky about your subject, too.

4. If you're going to use the electronic equipment that's advertised as being so simple a child could use it, it's probably true. Kids can operate anything these days. It's the adults who fumble and falter. Take your kid, or take an electronics technician.

5. Getting some of the new electronic equipment through security screens at major airports can be frazzling. Check with the airport *before* you go.

6. If you're counting on some stranger in the control room to help you, make sure you give him (or her) a crystal-clear cue sheet so that all of your splendid effects go on when you want them on. If you're expecting a stranger to recognize your cues from the stage, you're expecting a degree of mind reading that probably doesn't exist.

◄ 48 ►

Hostile Audiences

Hostile audiences can be nasty at times, but in all likelihood, the speaker has had nothing to do with it.

So, you may say, why are they hostile?

See if any of these sound familiar.

◄ It's not the group. It's *one* person in the group. Maybe that one person thinks she should have been promoted recently, but she was told she didn't show enough assertiveness. She's decided to demonstrate her assertiveness on you.

◄ The audience works for one boss who is in the room. The audience isn't crazy about the boss because he has shown himself to be very insensitive to the volume of work going through. They're mentally and physically exhausted. Now he has instructed them to listen to you.

◄ The audience is mad because a lot of people have been fired recently. You're innocent, of course, but the audience is in a mood to take out their resentment on somebody. Don't be surprised if it's you.

◄ The supervisor of the group is having trouble at home. When he's having trouble at home, he makes everybody miserable in the office. You caught one of the stormy times.

The point is simple, but difficult to accept. In most cases, the speaker is an innocent victim of the hostility—but, still, the speaker must deal with it. One solution that usually works is on the next page.

Taming the Hostile Audience

The secret of defanging a hostile audience is the old-fashioned bargain. *You do this . . . I'll do this.* Make it as simple and straightforward as possible:

"You were chosen to take part here today because this subject is important to your job. If you want to listen . . . hey, that's fine. If you want to get involved in a discussion, that's fine, too—but I'm sure you'll understand that we have to stay in some kind of time frame. After all, you have work to do—just like I have mine.

"Here's the deal: I promise you to have you out of here within an hour. I can also promise you some interesting ideas that you are free to accept or not. It's your call. It's my call to control the time. Just give me an open mind for the next fifty-five minutes. Can we strike a bargain on that?"

BE SURE TO GET A VOTE ON THAT QUESTION—A SHOW OF HANDS, WHATEVER. SOMETHING THAT EVERYBODY CAN WITNESS.

If you don't think you can get past that vote, you've got a *real* problem and would be best advised to close out as quickly as your self-respect will allow. However, once you've got the group quiet enough to hear your bargain, you're not likely to get more static. Cool heads usually respond favorably to such things as straight-shooter bargains and honest votes.

Now you can proceed quickly—since you know who is most likely to cause trouble, what subjects are sensitive, and you have an approved "treaty" that gives you full license to move things toward a specific ending.

Often, an outbreak of hostility—quieted by an agreement of sorts—will change the entire atmosphere for the rest of the meeting. And hostility will be replaced by cooperation, even—if you're lucky—congeniality.

◄ 50 ►
Orville Crabb

Orville Crabb was the most belligerent person I have ever seen in an audience.

He interrupted a presentation with these words, "Look ... I read your material at home, and I think you're full of ———."

It's hard to know what to say when a total stranger fires these words across your bow.

I concluded there are three things you might do:

1. Give in to your emotions and tell Orville Crab what he's full of. This can be very satisfying to the psyche, but hard on relationships, especially if Orville Crabb happens to be a client or a new business prospect.

2. Tell him he has just made a very interesting observation and you'd like to discuss it with him right after the meeting. This is an admirable response, and very good if you're presenting under a tight deadline (as was the case in this instance).

3. Tell him you appreciate his candor, and you would like to know exactly why he feels as he does. This could turn up some interesting comments. It could also get you into a discussion that might drag you even further into the muck.

The conditions of the situation dictate which answer is best. The truth of the matter is, you probably want to get away from the guy as quickly as possible—but there's no sense in being as nasty as he is. I'd give him #2 and hope he doesn't wait for you after the meeting.

51
The Lonely Last Speaker

Always ask to see a copy of the program *before* you take off for the conference. If you are the *last* speaker in a *three-day* conference—your audience is going to be flying home as you're mounting the speaker's platform. Tell your host you'd like an earlier slot or you'll have to stay an extra day. The schedule will open up for you like the Red Sea.

III

Tell Fear to Go Jump in the Lake, You've Got a Speech to Make

Some speakers visualize their audiences naked in order to overcome nervousness. It's effective, but distracting. Here are some other ways.

◄ 52 ►
Move!

Don't stand there like a statue, *move*! Nervousness hates a moving body.

◄ 53 ►
Clasp Your Hands

Want to know if you're really nervous? Clasp the palms of your hands together. How do they feel? If your skin feels chilly, your circulation is slowing because of pressure on your arterial system. The reason: plain old nervousness. What to do? Get your body moving. Trot around the block. Do some sit-ups. Try some windmills. You'll feel the warmth coming back to your skin—and your confidence will come with it.

◄ 54 ►
Nervousness Remedy #1

There's one surefire remedy for nervousness that makes all the others seem frivolous. You've got to prepare yourself so thoroughly that *nothing* will cause you to lose you focus and become unglued. Have at least *seven* times more information than you will actually use. When you say to yourself, "I know more about this subject than anyone else in the room," it should be true—not just *hopefully* true. When you're convinced it's true, you won't be nervous.

◄ 55 ►
One Friendly Face

When you gaze out over your audience, know where you can find at least one friendly face.

Alert the friend that you may need him or her during your presentation. Then, don't hesitate to look directly at that friendly face when you need some good vibes—or when your nerves are acting up. You'll be amazed at the calming effect of *one* friendly face when you're trying to connect with a sea of strangers.

◄ 56 ►
What They Don't Know—

If you're nervous, don't tell anybody. Most importantly, don't tell your audience. Most people won't be aware of it—and the others don't really want to know.

Audiences want to think of you as being totally in control of your presentation. Don't volunteer any reason for them to think otherwise.

◄ 57 ►

You Must Have a Safety Net

A safety net is something that can catch you if you start to fall. A safety net isn't going to help if you have some kind of gastric upset, or you lose your contact lenses.

But it can help if your memory decides not to show up on speech day.

You've got to have something in reserve that will keep your mouth moving until your mind kicks back in. Plan your safety net during rehearsal. Make sure it will work if needed.

Some speakers use their audiovisual aids as "notes."

When they expose a chart or a board, it reminds them of an important point they want to make. What the audience regards as an aid for them is really a safety net for the speaker.

A TelePrompTer is a safety net of sorts. It doesn't have to be programmed to provide you with the exact script. It can lead you with "cues" that give you much more freedom.

Symbolic maps of all kinds can be used. I suggested a Palm Map in my book called *Say It in Six*. You just hold it in the palm of your hand and refer to it if necessary. It's composed of pictures and charts rather than words. It's easier to see if you need it, and it communicates faster.

If you're on a platform above the audience, you can scatter sheets around the floor with big "trigger" words on them. Look down and the words "trigger" the thoughts that had eluded you. The audience doesn't know the words are there—but they flash instantly in your brain.

If you've got your presentation well prepared and well rehearsed, you'll probably never use your safety net. But here's the key: Just knowing it's there, ready and waiting to be of aid, can be enough to keep your nerves just where you want them . . . safely under your control.

◄ 58 ►
Avoiding a Nervous Breakdown

One of the major causes of nervousness is the fear that your audiovisual equipment will break down and you'll be left up there on the stage looking like a kid who lost his bicycle.

The answer is simple: Be able to sail right through *without* your AV stuff. You won't worry about a breakdown, and your nerves won't either.

Nervousness:
Strange Mannerisms

Some presenters earnestly believe that if they *look* relaxed while speaking—nervousness will avoid them.

I have seen a middle-aged man speaking to a fairly large audience with his hands interlaced behind his head. He kept them there, throughout his speech, as if being robbed.

When I asked him about it later, he claimed no recollection of doing any such thing.

I have seen speakers cross their arms *and* their legs, looking a bit like pretzels. Other presenters will brush one foot back and forth across the floor, as if practicing a dance step. They don't remember anything of the kind.

These mannerisms, I have concluded, are often a product of nervousness rather than ways to avoid it.

Here's a rule that you can safely follow: Anything you do *before* speaking (like deep breathing) is okay, and probably works. Anything you do to look relaxed *while* speaking is probably not going to work and will end up making you look goofy.

◄ 60 ►
Good Luck

Have a good luck charm that keeps nervousness away. It can be anything that calms your nerves. Doesn't matter how crazy it is as long as you're convinced *it works*.

IV

"Stargazing"

- ◄ Michael Jordan
- ◄ Bob Dole
- ◄ Don Imus
- ◄ Johnnie Cochran
- ◄ Sam Walton
- ◄ Senator Paul Simon
- ◄ Jason Robards
- ◄ Elizabeth Taylor
- ◄ Ruth Gordon
- ◄ Bobby Knight

With the media beaming celebrities at us twenty-four hours a day, you can learn a lot about presenting yourself by just keeping your eyes open.

◄ 61 ►
Michael Jordan

Outside of Chicago's United Center, a bronze statue flies through the air.

It is called "The Spirit," and though it weighs two thousand pounds, it captures the world's greatest basketball player *in full flight*.

In awe of his almost magical powers, kids pitch pennies at the base of the statue and make wishes to "Be Like Mike." Other fans, somewhat older, have been seen kneeling near the statue and praying.

Michael Jordan, besides being a winner, *connects* with audiences in a way that few athletes and/or celebrities ever have. People literally adore him, buying whatever he endorses. He presents himself with immaculate skill, speaking for the team—but clearly for much more than that, a leader who transcends athletics.

His techniques of communication (keep your poise under all conditions; avoid the clichés that seem to dog all professional athletes; maintain an aura of dignity; practice a sense of fair play no matter what the opposition does) are skills that take time to perfect, but there is one "ritual" which Michael freely admits to, and you can adopt it today—even if you've never touched a basketball. Here it is, from a recent article in *Esquire* magazine. They are Michael's words:

"My ritual is the same before every game. I wear a different pair of shoes every night. When I explain why, everyone can relate. Anybody who goes out and buys something new, let's say a new suit, you feel good about it. I wanted to feel that way every night."

So, Michael laces up a new pair of shoes before every game (he says he likes them tight) *and soars*.

If you can't afford a new pair of shoes before every presentation, how about a new necktie? Or a silk scarf by your favorite designer? Or a pair of earrings? Or whatever makes you feel good? Get it and wear it for your next presentation.

Oh, it's just a silly superstition, you say. Well, maybe. But it seems to work. Stand outside the United Center some night and notice how many people *connect* with Michael Jordan.

◄ 62 ►
Bob Dole

They say it was the day that Bob Dole came of age as a platform speaker. He was seventy-two, and he announced his resignation from the Congress after twenty-seven years of service in the U.S. Senate and eight years in the House.

He spoke more slowly than usual, and his words registered with greater impact. His script was better (he had a new writer). And he used a TelePrompTer for the first time in anybody's memory.

But there was something else.

He didn't seem to drone on and on—grinding out the words, as he usually did. He was different. There was a reason, and it dawned on people only when Bob Dole had finished.

He spoke for only six minutes.

◄ 63 ►

The Age of Imus

We live in a curious age where people can be entertained by hearing other people ridiculed. Human tragedies often become the grist of grisly jokes on late-night comedy.

Don Imus, the syndicated radio commentator of sorts, loves to get off a rip or two at sitting presidents and other notables. Audiences gasp and chuckle—just as long their names aren't mentioned in the skewering.

But it doesn't work unless you're a national personality who's expected to be shocking. It's a *very* narrow niche.

Don't even *think* about trying it.

‹ 64 ›
Johnnie Cochran

I've been trying to forget the O.J. Simpson trial, but one picture keeps developing itself over and over in my mind.

It is Defense Attorney Johnnie Cochran delivering his summation to the jury. He is wearing a dark stocking cap pulled down tight over his head. The cap was a piece of prosecution evidence, but it didn't look very dangerous on Johnnie.

As he stood there, speaking in his warm, textured voice, I thought to myself—I have a stocking cap like that. Just exactly like that.

The cap made me look at the defense attorney somewhat differently, more like myself—watching from Chicago—than someone who defends Hollywood stars in murder trials. Moreover, it made me see the cap in an environment totally different from the dark scene where the prosecution would have preferred that I remember it.

And the most compelling part of this whole picture is that it is locked in my brain forever. Images have a way of doing that. Never underestimate the power of a vivid image to make linkages in the mind that words alone simply cannot accomplish.

◄ 65 ►
Sam Walton

Make friends with your eyes. Sam Walton, the founder of Wal-Mart said, *"You look 'em right in the eye* and say, 'How can I help you today?' "* When he died, he was the richest man in America.

◄ 66 ►
Senator Paul Simon

Two experts are seated in the studio of the *News Hour with Jim Lehrer* (PBS). The host is in the middle, turning first to one expert and then the other, asking questions.

The first expert is answering a question. The second expert is itching to break in. Finally, he can contain himself no longer.

"I disagree with that. To me, that point of view just makes no sense at all. . . ."

The first expert shakes his head, looking down at the table. He seems visibly wounded. He isn't really listening to the other expert now. He is thinking about what he's going to say next that will *prove* he was right all along.

There's an important point here:

Never say another person is wrong. It's diminishing. It hurts. It usually starts a battle.

When Paul Simon was a senator from Illinois, he knew how to handle people who would dare to say he was wrong.

He has a big, baritone voice that would envelop a room. He'd smile slightly and rivet his opponent with a laser gaze.

"Let me see if I can help you with this," he'd say kindly. "There are two ways to consider the matter. The way you just mentioned—and a way that starts from a slightly different base." He'd continue on with his pleasant voice—outlining the second way that was totally at odds with the opinion on the other side of the table.

Simon always *depersonalized* the issue. He never contradicted the other person. He just looked at it differently, under the guise of making it clear to everybody.

Most TV "talk shows" like to create friction. But, in business, affairs of state, and other civilized forums, it's far better to ease into a contradictory point of view *without* labeling it as such. You'll also get more time to speak without being hassled.

◄ 67 ►
Jason Robards

Jason Robards made a wonderful quote for actors recently. Here's what he said:

"It takes years of hamming it up to even begin to do less."

Think about that. Here it is, same thought, for speakers:

You've got to work your way through the long night of being self-conscious before audiences will begin to believe that you are genuinely interested in them.

◄ 68 ►
Elizabeth Taylor

Be wary of presenting satires. The audience usually doesn't know if you're playing it straight or poking fun.

Maybe you noticed Elizabeth Taylor walking through a string of sitcoms one winter's night not long ago. She appeared to be a character in each story. She was *treated* like a character. But, on closer inspection, she had something else in mind. She was pitching her new perfume—as a part of the plot line. It was like an infomercial that would not stop.

Advertising's latest ploy is to befuddle. To put the product where you'd least expect it. Or, to ridicule it rather than praise it. But that's what *satires* do. So if advertising is a satire, how do you—the presenter—satirize the satirization?

It's just too confusing to be taken seriously. Leave satires to the satirists. Even they may wonder what's going on these days.

◄ 69 ►
Ruth Gordon

Here's an idea that breaks through all of the nervousness, all of the ponderous introductions, all of the twaddle that usually accompanies getting a speech off the ground:

If you're the speaker, just say something that has always intrigued you. Here's an example:

How old would you be if you didn't know how old you were?

Coming out of the blue, you've got their attention (everybody thinks about age).

Follow up any way you want. I usually say, "I've been forty-four for the past seven years."

Almost everybody has a favorite line about life. What's yours? Say it, and you've shown your humanity. Most importantly, you've broken through that brain-numbing wall of skepticism that always faces a speaker who has been laboriously introduced.

PS: If you use the quote on the preceding page, you might credit Ruth Gordon, the actress and author, who asked that question about herself and corralled a lot of readers in the process.

◄ 70 ►

Nobody Argues with Bobby Knight

They say great presentation is 80 percent preparation and 20 percent sheer animal energy.

Or, as Indiana's basketball coach Bobby Knight says, "Everybody has the will to win, precious few have the will to *prepare* to win."

V

"Ninety Seconds and Counting"

You're next up. Here are a few last-minute suggestions to clear the brain and calm the nerves.

‹ 71 ›
Humble Pie

Some speakers acknowledge their introductions by eating humble pie. You've heard the words a thousand times:

"I am sure there are many people in this audience today who know *much* more about this subject than I will ever know."

There are at least twenty seconds of this humbling routine, but that's the gist of it.

It is *not* a smart way to get on the good side of an audience.

If the statement is true—and not just humbug—then it raises questions about the guy who invited the speaker. In other words, if there are a lot of people who know more about the subject than the speaker, why weren't *they* invited?

If the statement is false—pure humbug—then what's the point in casting doubt on your own reputation *and* taking the edge off of the expectations of the audience?

Here's the bottom line: Most people know that introductions are roughly half fact and half fiction. So don't worry about what's said in your introduction unless it's some kind of egregious error that must not stand. Correct it "for the record" and move along. Another good, general rule: Honor the formalities, but don't embellish them. Nobody will remember them anyway.

◄ 72 ►

Never Trust a Stage Setter

Beware of introducers who say, "Just give me a few words to get you started. I don't know what I'll say—but I'll just set the stage for you. Trust me."

Don't.

He'll take five or six minutes to say nothing and probably mispronounce your name.

◄ 73 ►

Props are Cues—and Other Things

The more complex the subject you are presenting, the more likely that props will serve you in all kinds of ways. If your audience can see the props you have presented as you have worked your way through a technical subject, each prop becomes a reminder of the material just covered. At the end of your presentation, the props—laid out neatly on a table or display panel—become a table of contents to refresh the memory of the audience.

Thus, props serve the audience.

They serve the presenter as well. If you lose your way as you're speaking, glance over at your props and—if they're positioned in the order of use—you'll know exactly where you are.

Also, props just make you more interesting. Compare a speaker standing erect on a barren stage with one who is surrounded by props, picking them up one by one to show you which ones are hot investments—and why.

Which speaker would you watch?

◄ 74 ►
"But What About Those Germs?"

Never get up and apologize. "Please forgive me for this chest cold I've picked up somewhere." Immediately, the audience starts wondering how many million bronchial germs are filling the room.

Audiences don't want to worry about you. More to the point, they don't want to worry about themselves.

‹ 75 ›
How's the Air?

Your speech can be no better than the ventilating system in the room where you're speaking.

If the room is stuffy, you're likely to be regarded in the same way.

‹ 76 ›
Handouts

Beware of giving handouts to your audience before you speak. You are inviting them to pay *zero* attention to your speech.

‹ 77 ›
Reaching Out

Every speech, no matter how long or how short, wants to *convert* the audience. Every speaker wants the audience to eventually shout a rousing "*Yes!*" to the idea being proposed.

That simply provides a necessary and positive closure to the speech.

But what happens if you don't feel that moment of closure?

You've got to have enough flexibility in your speech to reach out to your audience and find out exactly what's happening.

Here are two things you can do:

◄ Have a little role-playing fun. Ask them to "act out" the gist of your subject. If they do it with alacrity, you've made your point. If they just look at you, you've got repair work to do.

◄ Throw a few review questions around the room. See if your audience perks up and competes to answer. If you get nothing but silence, you've missed connections.

Here's the point: Most speakers just rumble through a speech and sit down. Did the audience get it? Who knows? Your speech must provide some "windows" for you to see what has actually happened inside the minds of your audience. It's like adding up your score on the golf course. If you don't do it, you haven't really played the game.

◄ 78 ►

Be Like George

Don't read your speech.

It will make the audience wonder who wrote it.

It will sound phony—not like real people talk.

It will prevent eye contact; the most powerful tool a speaker can use.

It will keep you pinned down to a lectern.

If you leave the script to add a few spontaneous words of your own, you'll have a devil of a time trying to find your way back in.

*

Use a few notes if you must. George Carlin does, and people pay $40 a ticket to hear him.

◄ 79 ►
Overheard at Church

"He gives the best sermons I have ever heard. They touch me to the quick. But he has never once looked me directly in the eye. I pray that he will. Until he does, I will continue to believe that his glorious words of inspiration and enlightenment are meant for someone else."

◄ 80 ►
Your Half

If you're speaking to a half-filled room, make sure the half that's filled is sitting *close to you*.

◄ 81 ►
Me? Jangle?

Get rid of loose metal before you begin. You have no idea how many people jangle coins or chunky jewelry during a speech and then say, "Me? Jangle? No. Not *me*."

◄ 82 ►
A Structure That Never Falls

This is quite possibly the best speech structure in the world for the speaker who has ninety seconds before "speaking time" and his or her mind has turned to mush:

◄ Say It.
◄ Show It.
◄ Sum It Up.

VI

Time Out
for Three
Short Stories

All true, all personal, all with one aim: to help you win an ovation at your next presentation.

‹ 83 ›

"Akron,
I'll Never Forget You"

It was close to the very first speech I ever made—and I was obsessed with its preparation. I feel a case of nerves just thinking about it now.

I had been invited to address the Akron Advertising Club by my good friend, Jack Houlette. He was the advertising manager of one of the big rubber companies headquartered in Akron. He was also program chairman at the Ad Club and he needed a speaker. I felt complimented to be asked, but I neglected to tell him I that I was a neophyte.

Frankly, I don't recall my subject—but advertising must have had something to do with it. I accumulated a massive, unruly manuscript and worked long hours editing it down to size.

On the day of my speech, I showed up in Akron in a spiffy new suit, topped off with a bright red necktie. I felt loose. Jack was my shepherd, and the crowd was loud and friendly.

After lunch and all of the local announcements, I was introduced as "an advertising executive from New York." (I was a copywriter.)

The speech came easily to mind—sentence by sentence—as if everything was preformed and marked for placement. After a while, I just seemed to float—never reaching for thoughts—just expecting them to be there.

I sat down to courteous applause.

Jack got up and seemed somewhat at a loss for words. Finally, "Well, we all owe Ron a vote of thanks for giving us quite a speech today ... (ANOTHER MODEST ROUND OF APPLAUSE) ... *and to think that he memorized the entire thing.*"

*

Every compliment that I received later was about the fact that I had memorized the whole speech.

I learned two things that day that seem worthy of passing along to you:

1. Don't let yourself become so immersed in a subject that your brain *locks* the words behind the walls of your memory like a flood behind a dam.

2. When an audience is so impressed by your ability to memorize that it pays no attention to your subject, you really haven't connected in a way you'd like to remember.

◂ 84 ▸
"Teaching Tough"

This is a true story, with an important lesson I've never heard expressed before.

I was in New Orleans at a small but diligent advertising agency. It had been founded by two decent, hardworking people who eventually became CEO and president.

They were going after a sizable chunk of new business. A three-million-dollar account—and they *had* to win it. Their cash flow was sluggish and they hadn't won a new account in eight months. (That's a long drought in the agency business.)

I watched the two of them rehearse their presentation all day. Even the most generous coach would have said they were pathetic. They had done a ton of work, but it didn't really connect. However, I was told that my mission was to improve their delivery—which was so low-key that I wondered how they had ever gotten anybody's attention. I tried to help, but it was like pushing an elephant uphill. I knew there was bound to be a saber-toothed tiger out there in New Orleans somewhere who would have my clients for lunch.

During the plane ride back to Chicago, the valiant little agency in New Orleans stayed in mind. On the next day, I was to teach a group of bright, young, international trainees who had been selected to take a ten-day development course in Chicago. I was to teach one day of presentation skills. With memories of the embattled New Orleans executives still in mind, I decided that the future of these young trainees depended upon their not turning out like my hapless friends in New Orleans. *They must learn how to win new business.*

The next day, I addressed the group like Mike Ditka giving a pep talk to his beloved Bears. I spoke with coachlike fervor, telling them how valuable the day was going to be. I then split them into groups and made them compete against each other—presenting over and over until they were exhausted. But I sensed they were slowly learning. They were turning into tigers.

At the end of the day, the group dispersed with what I saw as a look of weary gratitude.

The next day, I returned and wandered through the halls, listening for comments. There were none. Later I saw the evaluations by the trainees of my one-day training session.

"Brutal," "Learned a few things—but it was no fun." "Too serious—too much talk about winning and losing." "Whew! Too intense." "It was like a rugby scrimmage."

The comments disappointed me, but I learned some things I wouldn't have acknowledged any other way:

You can't move in for one day and assume that you're going to transform people. You can't conduct a "boot camp" for one day. People may like intensity in their presentations, but not a tornado that whirls into their midst for one day and moves on.

Ever since then (approximately ten years ago), I don't try to evangelize audiences—no matter how strongly I feel about the subject. I've learned that audiences want their wisdom doled out with ample helpings of fun and good-heartedness.

If you're going to be Mike Ditka, give yourself enough time to build a relationship with your team—so that they know what to expect.

Even then, "teaching tough" is a hard row to hoe. Mike hasn't found a coaching job since he left the Bears, over four years ago.

◄ 85 ►

The Fate of
the Fifty Percenter

Recently, I was conducting a marketing seminar in New York City. I asked a senior member of the firm, "When you're presenting an idea to a client, what percentage of the time do you really believe in it?"

"What do you mean?" he asked.

"Well, how often do you feel so strongly about the idea that you would invest your own money in it?"

"Oh, about fifty percent of the time," he said.

"What about the other fifty percent?" I asked.

"I don't know," he said. "I guess I just have to push myself a little harder."

*

No wonder we have so many plays and movies about down-hearted salesmen, so many jokes about overly accommodating attorneys.

If you are trying to put across an idea, but you don't believe in it yourself, you're in for some very rough sledding. When the presenter is merely going through the motions—representing a cause rather than believing in it—then it's time to find someone who *does* believe, even if the delivery is less polished.

Sincerity and conviction will always beat flamboyance.

VII

"Put on Your Suit of Lights— and Sally Forth."

You've readied yourself. *Now, it's the time to care for* them.

◄ 86 ►
How to Start

1. Be prepared. Move swiftly. Act like you can hardly wait to get started.
2. Head for your mark on the floor. It should be a spot where no speaker has stood before.
3. Look around. Let them know by your expression that you have just taken charge of the room. It is yours, every cubic foot of it, for as long as your speech will last.
4. Find a friend. Smile. Step forward.
5. Say something that's easy for you to say and makes you feel comfortable (see "Ruth Gordon" in Part 4).

◄ 87 ►
"You're Really Going to Get a Kick Out of This . . ."

Don't tell your audience how much they're going to enjoy the joke you're about to tell them.

Audiences prefer to make up their own minds about humor.

Tell a *true story* that relates directly to your subject. If you get a laugh, rejoice. If you don't, no need to give the slightest indication that you expected one.

◄ 88 ►
Over Their Heads?

Many audiences "tune out" of a presentation because the language of the speaker travels *miles* above their heads. They go into information overload and *disconnect.*

You can almost feel the tune-out moment when it happens. Eyes glaze over and become fixed in space. Legs and arms turn away from the speaker. Postures droop as if to say, "Don't look my way—*I'm lost.*"

The remedy? Stop and summarize what you've been trying to communicate. Write your main points—four or five words per point—on a jumbo pad or greenboard where everybody can see them. Move into your audience. Show by your body language that you're aware of what's happened—and you're ready to speak *their* language.

Most important, burn these words into your consciousness: *It is impossible to be too clear.*

‹ 89 ›
Charge!

There's a difference between a verbal essay and a compelling presentation. A verbal essay leaves you informed but unmoved. A compelling presentation leaves you *converted*. You are ready to get on your horse and *charge!*

‹ 90 ›
The Eyes Have It

If you don't make eye contact, you might as well put it on E-mail and post it in the Forum.

‹ 91 ›
Call an Audible

Don't get locked into a script. Let your audience guide you as you speak.

Here's what I mean: Audiences are constantly reacting. Maybe they're restless. Maybe they're worn out. Maybe you've lost them.

If you keep the lights up, you can see what your audience is telling you. You can see it in their facial expressions. You can see it in their body language.

An attentive speaker reacts, *immediately*.

Be ready to "call an audible" on yourself. Calling an audible simply means adjusting to the way your audience is behaving.

Maybe you call a break. Maybe you leave your script. Maybe you change subjects abruptly.

The crucial point: Don't let yourself get isolated from your audience. You can feel it when it happens. Adjust. Do what you feel is necessary.

Call an audible and take action.

Remember . . . when you present, you lead.

◄ 92 ►
You? Rattled? Never!

If a distraction occurs as you're speaking, acknowledge it:

- *Phone rings:* "Could you get that?" (spoken to person nearest to phone).
- *Plate crashes in kitchen:* "Oh, oh . . . get his serial number . . ."

◄ *Waiter comes into meeting room to take luncheon order:* "Could you come back in five minutes? I'll have this wrapped up by then."

◄ *Jackhammer starts pounding outside window:* "I'm going to pretend I don't hear that. If it gets to be too much for you, let me know."

The bottom line: Always let your audience know you're not bothered by the distraction and they needn't be, either.

93
Take Your Watch Off

Never look at your watch when you're speaking.

President Bush did this during the 1992 election campaign. He was debating with Bill Clinton and Ross Perot at the time.

Nobody remembers any points that Bush made during that debate. But nobody forgot him taking a long look at his watch. He wasn't speaking at the time, but his message was clear: "I'm sick of this and I want to go home."

VIII

"Who's Got the First Question?"

This is the most perilous part of any speech. The audience is going to test you—and confrontation is always lurking in the weeds.

◄ 94 ►
Step into Every Question and Smile

... "stepping in" (literally stepping toward your questioner) shows that you're prepared and confident.

... "and smile," not a big, toothpaste smile—just a pleasant expression that contributes to a friendly atmosphere.

In Q & A, body language talks louder than words.

◄ 95 ►
Q & A Hazards

The Q & A section of your presentation can be fraught with peril. Here's why:

1. Your audience is *participating*—maybe "showing off" in front of its peers.
2. Your audience may have its own agenda that is very different from yours.

3. Your audience may be testing you—asking questions that they know how to answer, but are doubtful if you do.

4. Don't be tempted to guess! There's nothing wrong with saying, "Hey, you caught me on that one—I'll have the answer *in writing* on your desk by ten o'clock tomorrow morning."

◄ 96 ►
No Questions? How Come?

Why? Why on earth wasn't there at least *one* question? Here are some possibilities:

1. Your presentation answered every single question. (A rare occurrence, but possible.)

2. Your presentation was headed into "dangerous waters" and your audience was content to let matters rest.

3. Your audience was eager to move on. Your presentation was okay, but too long.

4. Hey, let's face it. You picked a subject in which your audience had absolutely no interest.

5. You *overwhelmed* them with data. It was good, but it was just *too much*.

6. Your audience lost the thread of your presentation about halfway through.

7. The headwaiter just arrived to take the luncheon order.

◄ 97 ►
What Is a Question?

There's only one way to think of a question. It is a genuine expression of further interest in what you have to say. Questions are to be welcomed with open arms, as avenues to further information that can be useful to all concerned.

Some presenters think of questions as *objections*. This is a sure route to argumentation. It may work in a murder trial, but never in a business meeting.

◄ 98 ►
Listening Hard

The harder you listen, the more intently you soak up the questioner's comment or query—the more likely your response will be accepted.

It's this simple: People want to believe that their views have *really* been heard and considered.

It is astonishingly rare.

All too often I get the impression that while the questioner is pouring out his/her side of the matter, the person who will answer is simply waiting for the question to end.

You must show a respect for the question *and* the questioner before you can expect your answer to be regarded in the same way.

◄ 99 ►
Questions That Keep Coming Back

If you are going to face this audience again, make sure that someone writes down every question that's asked. Questions tell you a lot about what's important to your audience.

◄ 100 ►
Believe the Eyes

Watch their eyes as you answer their questions. If they really *listen*—that is, their eyes never leave yours as you speak—you're converting them to your point of view.

If they're frowning or looking away, they aren't buying your answer. They're busy raising barriers.

If they close their eyes to your answer, they are trying to shut it out of their minds. They *hate* it.

If they nod "okay"—ever so slightly—you have answered satisfactorily.

If the eyes say "no" when the voice says "okay"—believe the eyes.

◄ 101 ►
Time Out

Here is the best answer to an impolite or surly question:

"Gee, that's a question I really hadn't expected.
Give me a couple of minutes to think about it."

Nobody will turn down that request: It will give you time to gather your thoughts—and it may give your questioner time to forget what he asked in the first place.

Steal the President's Secrets

Use the Presidential Press Conference technique of answering questions. *Anticipate* the questions that will be asked (people ask about issues that are closest to their own responsibilities). You will guess right on 70 percent of the questions you have anticipated. The President of the United States allows 150 words for each question, and has a "capper" ready for each question. A "capper" confirms the original answer and usually tops it off with a bit of humor.

◄ 103 ►

*"In Light of Your Previous Actions,
How Can You Expect Us Ever to
Trust You Again?"*

This was a question asked of President Clinton by a complete stranger at a town meeting in Wichita, Kansas, on April 4, 1994.

Moral: Even when you get to be President of the United States, you're never safe from a verbal poke in the eye. *Idea*: Think of the six *meanest* questions you could get, then have your answers mostly memorized. Leave a little room for customizing. You will answer so beautifully that you will forget to feel annoyed about the question.

◄ 104 ►
Come Back to the Core

When answering questions, always come back to the core. The core is the simple, discrete message you want your audience to take action on.

"Yes, it will take a year to build the new stadium, but it will provide work for ten thousand people—maybe even members of your family. That alone should be worth a YES vote next Tuesday."

IX

"Thank You for Inviting Me Today"

How did you do? How do you feel? Before you answer, consider a few words from Tennessee Williams.

◄ 105 ►
Tennessee Williams Time

You'll always know when you have made a great speech. You'll hear it in the crispness of the applause. You'll see it in the big smiles. Best of all, you'll feel it inside yourself.

If you *haven't* connected, the applause will be perfunctory. The crowd will mill about and ask about the next speaker. Never mind. You've already started making your mental list of what worked and what didn't. So you're bound to be better next time.

Whichever way it goes, I call this Tennessee Williams Time. He's the playwright who had his share of hits and misses, but his attitude toward life never changed. . . .

◄ 106 ►
"Life Is a Journey. Take It!"
—*Tennessee Williams*

Congratulations, my friend, you've covered quite a few miles today.

◄ Epilogue ►
A Few Nuggets to Take Personally

◄ One of the nicest comments I ever heard about making presentations was made by a woman in North Dakota. She stood up and said, "You know, the most remarkable thing about speaking to people is that it's easy if you just go by the rules of decent behavior. If you treat an audience like you would a real good friend, you'll do all right as a speaker."

◄ Don't take all of the handbooks and manuals too seriously. They mean well, but they can take all the fun out. Take some risks. Develop your own style. Feel the naked joy of speaking fearlessly.

◄ Set a goal for yourself as a speech-maker: *Win a standing ovation for your next speech*. If it should happen that you don't get a standing ovation next time, get one for the speech after that. I never made a hole in one, never won the lottery, but I did get *one* standing ovation. My one and only. It lifted me about ten feet off the floor. It was *glorious*. It occurred to me later that I had never known an audience better than I had known that one.

◄ Keep the lights up. Engage your audience. You will not only see how *they're* doing, you'll see how *you're* doing. Audiences are a mirror reflection of what they see in the speaker. If you are filled with joy, your audience will play it right back to you.

◄ You don't have to end by topping one high note with another high note. Only Kate Smith (remember her?) did that every time—and that was only when she sang "God Bless America." When you get to a point where you feel great about yourself and great about your audience, just say "Thank you very much, I've enjoyed it," and sit down. Your audience may be a bit startled, but I have yet to see an audience that was truly annoyed when a speaker made an honest decision that he or she just couldn't top that last high note.

Thank you very much, I've enjoyed it,

Ron Hoff